Crafting the *Perfect* College Essay

Write Your Best Essay in 3 Easy Steps

Martina E. Faulkner, LMSW

INSPIREBYTES
OMNI MEDIA

Crafting the *Perfect* College Essay

Copyright © 2020 Martina E. Faulkner
All rights reserved.

No part of this publication may be reproduced or transmitted in any form or by any means, electronic or mechanical, including photocopying, recording, or any information storage and retrieval system, without express permission in writing from the publisher.

Distributed globally with Expanded Distribution by KDP.

ISBN Paperback: 978-0-9963668-9-2
ISBN E-Book: 978-1-953445-90-2
Library of Congress Control Number: 2020943848

 Inspirebytes Omni Media

Inspirebytes Omni Media LLC
PO Box 988
Wilmette, IL 60091

For more information, please visit Inspirebytes.com.

I dedicate this book to all the aspiring
writers and storytellers in the world.

Table of Contents

Introduction	1
I. What Are They Really Asking?	9
II. Where to Start	15
III. Step 1: Analysis	23
IV. Step 2: Structure	31
V. Step 3: Story	39
VI. Tripping Yourself Up	45
VII. Putting It All Together	55
VIII. About Me and Why I Wrote This Book	57
Acknowledgements	63
Resources	65

Martina E. Faulkner LMSW

Introduction

How do you capture an admissions officer's attention in only 5 minutes with 500 words? For so many young writers, this becomes the stumbling block that makes writing college essays feel overwhelming—but it doesn't have to be. When you understand what's really going on, writing a memorable college essay takes only three steps.

In this book, I am going to share what you need to know to write your best college essay, or any other short format piece of writing you may need to do in the future. You'll get tips and ideas on how you can approach your writing with confidence so that you can be assured of a positive result.

Writing is both a talent and a skill. Skilled writing is developed by learning different techniques, joining a writing group, and working on the basics. The key to honing your skill is practice.

Writing talent is a little different. The writers who create gorgeous novels and worlds that take us on journeys beyond our imagination have some measure of talent. It's a gift to write like that. However, being able to write creatively includes knowing the basics, such as grammar and how to form sentences. Creative writing requires honing your skill as a writer. This means that no matter what type of writing you are doing, learning how to improve your writing skill is an integral piece of the puzzle.

Over the years, I have participated in numerous writing groups online that have given me access to a lot of other people's writing. I think the biggest mistake that people who want to be successful authors make is that they don't invest in learning how to write well. They think the "story" alone is good enough. Nothing could be further from the truth.

A good story is only as good as the skill it's built on. Without a strong foundation, the story gets lost. Why? Because it's not accessible to the audience. If a reader is tripping over grammatical mistakes and structural errors, they can never really get into the story, no matter how special it is. All of the errors become obstacles to their access and immersion.

One of my professors in graduate school, who is a best-selling author and could have shared any number of tips with us, shared only one. She said simply, "The best advice I can give you is to learn how to write well."

If you want to be successful, if you want to achieve your goals, if you want to create a future and a career in which you can grow and thrive and make your own way, learn how to write well. Nearly every profession requires some form of writing. Whether you are a scientist, a doctor, a coach, a teacher, a nurse, or even a comedian — being able to write well can only help you.

This is also true for writing your college essay.

So, where do we begin?

To start with, the biggest perspective shift you need to make is to know that when you're working on your college essay, you need to start with crafting, not writing. Writing comes in at the end. Crafting is about building. It's about collecting all the pieces before you start to make a sentence. Think of IKEA. Every box contains all the pieces you need to build whatever it is you purchased. Whether it's a bookcase, a chair, a desk, or a bed, the instructions are the same:

- Remove all the pieces from the box
- Lay them out on the floor and review the contents with the instruction manual
- Count everything to make sure it's complete
- Read the *entire* instruction manual before you begin
- Assemble the piece

In order to build a stable piece of flat-pack furniture, you need to familiarize yourself with all the pieces and understand where they go. You also have to build the piece in a specific order. If you build the sections out of order, there's no guarantee that it will work. If you ignore the instructions and just "wing it"—it's almost certain that something will go wrong.

This is true if it's your first piece of IKEA furniture. If, however, it's your 100th piece, you may be able to wing it a little more easily. Because you have familiarized yourself with the process, repeatedly, over time, you have a better understanding of how these things work and some of it will have become second nature.

Writing is exactly the same. Once you have been writing for a while, and the basics have become ingrained in your work, you can dive in and write something fairly effortlessly.

Why?

Because you put the work in on the front end to understand the core of writing and how everything fits together. You have developed and honed your writing skill. For example, do I always use an outline? No. But, do I know *how* and, more importantly, do I know *when* to use an outline? Yes. That's what honing your skill means. You understand both *how* and *when* to use the tools to best effect, and you practice them.

When you become accustomed to thinking a certain way—through all that practice—the outline is already in your head before you ever sit down and type. You write, and write, and write until you don't need an outline for every project—but you still know when it's important to use one.

That kind of practice, of course, takes time. For your college essays, we're not talking about becoming a best-selling novelist, nor do we have the time to hone your writing skill over months or years. What we're talking about is how to use the same tools great writers use to give you an essay you can be proud of and that an admissions officer will read and make them want to get to know you better.

These tools and steps are simple. In order to create—or craft—the best college essay, you have to lay out all the pieces, familiarize yourself with them, make a plan, and then go in a specific order to arrive at the best result. In this way, your writing will be cumulative as each step builds on the one prior.

This is especially important, because you may find that you change your entire approach by the time you arrive at the "writing" phase. When I first delivered this presentation and walked the participants through the process, this is exactly what happened, and it's only because we took the steps that the students were able to redirect their essays and focus on a topic that was much more powerful and tangible. The result? Instead of focusing on their original topics, the revised essays reflected an aspect of their life that was unique, which allowed their passion to come through. Here's one story:

> Emma was a senior high school swimmer who originally thought the focus of her essay would be on her personal accomplishments on the swim team. However, by the time we finished going through the three-step process, it turned out that what she wanted to focus on and write about was the camaraderie she felt on the team, not her personal accomplishments. What mattered most to her was that she felt part of something. She experienced a sense of belonging as a member of her team, and that was what allowed her to excel.
>
> Had she started writing as soon as she had the first idea, she would have written a decent essay about her successes, but she would not have tied her success to the sense of belonging. It was this insight that allowed her to write a much more compelling essay, and it was going through the three-step

process that made it possible. Not only was her new essay more compelling, but she had a lot more to say, which made the writing easier for her in the long run.

This process is exactly what I am outlining in this book. It's a process that makes any short format writing easier, especially college essays.

As you may be beginning to understand, not only is there a specific process, but there is also a specific order you need to follow to build a great essay. This approach will make you a better writer. It will also prevent you from having to spend a lot of time re-writing if your focus shifted as you went along, as did Emma's.

Personally, I dislike having to do something more than once, especially if there are tools that can prevent this. It's actually one of the reasons I came up with the program you're about to discover. As a professional writer, I wanted to share what I have learned over the years in a simple and accessible way. As a Certified Life Coach, I wanted to create a simple, yet tangible, tool that anyone could use to improve their writing skills, or at least their chances of being accepted into the college of their dreams.

What you're about to read is a really simple, yet effective approach to writing. My advice is to read everything before you begin. You need to understand all of the pieces before you start to put it together. If you need help, I also created a companion workbook that you can purchase and download immediately. It is filled with exercises for every step of the process to make it easier. It will definitely help you create your best essay and hone your writing skills.

Mostly, I wish you the best of luck and joy as you embark on this next chapter of your life. Now, let's move on and start working on learning how to craft that perfect essay!

What Are They Really Asking?

College essays typically focus on asking you to write about yourself from many different perspectives. Usually, they want to know who you are by asking you 'Who-What-Where-How-Why' questions. Some colleges ask more specific questions based on your area of interest. For example, the STEM (Science, Technology, Engineering, Math) departments often have additional essay requirements that are unique to that field of study.

For the purposes of this book, we're going to use the Common Application questions as a reference, because they are the most generalized. Additionally, they're the questions most people struggle with, simply because they are so generic. I have found that a lot of people have difficulty writing about themselves. This is true whether they are 17 or 47 years old.

In 2020-2021, the essay prompts are as follows:

> **The Common App 2020-2021 Essay Prompts**
>
> 1. Some students have a background, identity, or interest that is so meaningful that they believe their application would be incomplete without it. If this sounds like you, please share your story.
>
> 2. The lessons we take from obstacles we encounter can be fundamental to later success. Recount a time when you faced a challenge, setback, or failure. How did it affect you, and what did you learn from the experience?
>
> 3. Reflect on a time when you questioned or challenged a belief or idea. What prompted your thinking? What was the outcome?
>
> 4. Describe a problem you've solved or a problem you'd like to solve. It can be an intellectual challenge, a research query, an ethical dilemma - anything that is of personal importance, no matter the scale. Explain its significance to you and what steps you took or could be taken to identify a solution.
>
> 5. Discuss an accomplishment, event, or realization that sparked a period of personal growth and a new understanding of yourself or others.
>
> 6. Describe a topic, idea, or concept you find so engaging that it makes you lose all track of time. Why does it capitvate you? What or who do you turn to when you want to learn more?
>
> 7. Share an essay on a topic of your choice. It can be one you've already written, one that responds to a different prompt, or one of your own design.
>
> © 2020 The Common Application, Inc

For the previous years (2019-2020 and 2018-2019), the prompts were the same. In any given year, the Common Application will focus on asking questions along similar themes. They are all designed to give you an opportunity to introduce yourself to the admissions officer reviewing your application.

What is the benefit to using the Common Application? Time. You fill the application out once, check the boxes for where you want it to go, pay the necessary fees, and you're done. By using the Common Application, you don't have to write multiple applications—or essays—for every single school. This can make life easier for you. It also allows you to really hone in on writing one or two really excellent essays, instead of spreading yourself too thin by trying to write for all the different schools.

In looking at these specific prompts, there were some interesting statistics from 2018. Prompts #2, #5, and #7 were selected the most. Not surprisingly, #7 was first in that list, and here's why I think that is.

I think students (teenagers/seniors) are under so much pressure these days that it's easier to recycle something you have already written somewhere else and simply cut and paste it on your college application. The prompt essentially says: "share something on the topic of your choice that you could have used elsewhere."

Why wouldn't you choose this option? It's easy, right? And who doesn't like easy?

Well, I think once you learn the simple steps to crafting your college essay, you will *want* to write something new to put your best foot forward when applying to the college of your dreams. When you see how easy it is, you won't need to select Option #7.

Interestingly, the second-most popular prompt was #5, which shows that a lot of people are choosing to not take the easy way out and are crafting something new for this exact purpose. Prompt #5 asks you to write about "an accomplishment, event, or realization, that sparked a period of personal growth and a new understanding of yourself or others."

This is the most typical—and generic—college essay prompt. It asks you to write about you, without giving a whole lot of direction. It would seem that the sky's the limit here, right? Well, if you had 2,000 words, maybe. But since you have only about 500-600 words, you have to focus on what they're *really* asking you.

Look back at all the prompts: What do they have in common? That's the first question you need to ask yourself.

All of the Common Application prompts are asking you to write about *just one thing*. They don't want to know how your high school career went. They don't want to know how your involvement in a team sport went. They want to know about one specific thing that happened to you in a meaningful way and why it was meaningful. They want to know one specific thing that challenged you and what you did about it. Regardless of how it's phrased, that's what they're really asking.

More importantly, what every college application question is asking of you is to write an essay that says: "This is who I am—this is my character."

Some of the ways you can think about this is by asking yourself these questions:

- What am I passionate about? (i.e.: What makes my heart smile and motivates me?)

- Who has inspired me? (i.e.: Who in my life has made a big impact on me?)

- Why do I want to go to this college? (i.e.: What about this college makes me feel excited?)

- How have I grown as a person in high school? (i.e.: What positive change have I made from freshman to senior year?)

Writing about yourself doesn't have to be difficult. What makes it easier is understanding:

A. What the colleges are really asking, and
B. The steps to building the best essay.

Once you know the latter, you will be able to give them exactly what they really want, regardless of how they ask.

Crafting the Perfect College Essay

Where to Start

Before I begin any writing project, I ask the 'big picture' questions. I want to know what the overall goal is for the project, as well as any important information I might need to complete it. When I work as a ghostwriter, I create a lot of "homework" for my clients, in order to understand what's important and what's not. I can research almost anything, but I can't be inside my clients' minds if I don't ask a lot of questions first.

Think of taking a road trip. If you're starting at Point A and you want to get to Point B, you'd want to know a few things before you load up the car and hit the road. For starters, you'd need to know how long the trip is going to take. From that you would then need to assess stopping points, if necessary, as well as gas stations and road construction. If you've ever been stuck in summer road construction for miles with only a quarter of a tank of gas, you learn pretty quickly how important it is to get the big picture before you begin.

Similarly, if you've been driving on Highway 80 across Pennsylvania, you know that it can be 60 miles or more before the next exit, so you might not drink that iced tea as quickly.

Writing is the same. You need to know where you're starting and where you want to end in order to begin.

Understanding the Big Picture

As I've already mentioned with the IKEA example, you need to read everything and do every step before you actually begin crafting your essay. It's important. Otherwise, you might end up having to re-write things, and why do that if you don't have to?

So, let's start with the premise behind the program. Understanding how to craft your essay is about following three steps, in a specific order.

A simple and relevant mnemonic is your pathway to success. Actually, it's both an acronym and a mnemonic.

It's: E-S-S-A-Y.

    E = Everyone
    S = Story
    S = Structure
    A = Analysis
    Y = You

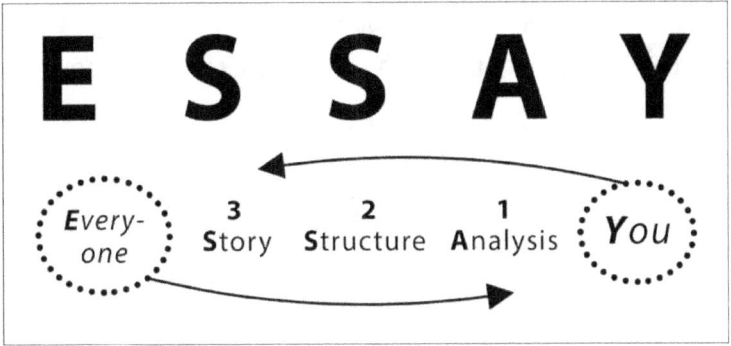

E is for Everyone. This is your audience. This is who is reading your essay. This represents everyone except you.

S is for Story. Story is the message you want Everyone to receive. You want Everyone to be able to read your story and get to know you, your character, and who you truly are.

S is for Structure. In order to tell a good Story, it has to have structure supporting it. This is both correct grammar and the actual building and placement of words, phrases, and sentences. This is what makes your Story accessible.

A is for Analysis. The Analysis is what gives you the basis for your Story. Analysis is where your Story has its roots. It allows Everyone to believe your Story.

Y is for You. Your Story begins with You. No two people can write exactly the same Story, because no two people will approach the Analysis, Structure, and Story in the same way. You make the Story unique. You are the reason for the Story.

Sometimes we need a metaphor to make things tangible in our brains. I like to use a house as the perfect metaphor for how to craft the perfect essay.

If you think of a house, Everyone represents all the people that drive by or live in the neighborhood. They will see a house and they will respond to what they see. The house itself tells a story of the people inside to everyone outside.

When someone drives by a house, they may notice the color of the house, the curb appeal or landscaping, and the windows and whether they have shades or curtains or shutters. If it's night time, people driving by may look into a house and see artwork on the walls, the color of the walls, what lamps someone has, or even where their bed is located and what their linens look like.

All of the information gathered by Everyone driving by a house is the Story. It's the decoration and the details. It's the little things that make one house different from another house on the same street. All of these choices tell a Story about the homeowner in one way or another.

What Everyone driving by doesn't see (unless it's in disrepair) is the infrastructure of the house. How are the walls built? Is the plumbing working? Have you ever driven by a house with a plumber's van out front and said to yourself, "Oh, they must be having an issue?" I know I have. When I drive by a home with work vans out front, I reflexively tell myself a story about why they're there.

When you see a house being built, you can actually see the infrastructure. But seeing the interior bones tells you nothing about the people who will be living there. The Structure alone has no Story. The Structure is the vehicle that carries the Story. It's what gives the Story something on which it can exist.

You wouldn't decorate a wall that was crumbling, would you? Similarly, you can't paint a Story on a wall that might fall down—though many people try.

Before the Structure is built, there has to be a foundation. In some parts of the country, this is a basement built below the frost line. In other parts of the country, this is a concrete slab. Whatever your foundation is, it has to be stable. That's the most important part. It's the basis for the entire house.

Similarly, your Analysis is the basis for your entire Story. Without Analysis, your story can just ramble on without any clear purpose or direction. Without a foundation, a house will fall apart. You can't hang shutters on a house that isn't properly rooted into the ground. Without Analysis, your Story may be interesting, but it won't be compelling.

Finally, there's You. You make the house a home. It's your personal touches and decorative choices that set your home apart from your neighbor's. Without You, a Story is just words on a page. You give it life, and you give it meaning. It's your Story. It needs You at its core.

This is the big picture of how to craft a perfect college essay. It requires all of these elements to be the best it can be, and they have to be constructed in a specific order. Otherwise, they will probably fall apart.

I think it's time for some real-life examples.

Previously I mentioned the various authors' groups I used to belong to. Well, let me tell you about one person whose book I started to read as a favor. This author couldn't understand why she wasn't successful yet, because she had "such a good story." She asked anyone in the group to read her book and give her honest feedback. I volunteered.

I read the first chapter of this author's work, and I stopped. I had read enough. This was a book she had self-published a year earlier, and it had sold less than one hundred copies. In the first chapter alone, there were more than 40 typos and grammatical errors. (Actually, I lost count; we will address the importance of editing later in the book.)

It's important to understand that even with the *best* story, structural issues in a book make it inaccessible to the reader. If a reader has to struggle to read your work because of errors and typos or rambling thoughts, they will never hear the message of your story.

The author from my group wasn't selling her work because she hadn't honed her craft. She didn't invest in the one thing she wanted more than anything: to be a successful writer. She believed that good writing is solely about the idea. A good idea is only a good idea if you can get others to buy into it. If it has developmental or structural issues, the likelihood of getting people to support it is low because they won't stick around long enough to hear it. In my experience, this is true across all industries.

The bottom line is that if you want to get an admissions officer to ask you to come for an interview, you have to put your best foot forward. In order to do that, you have to write a compelling, well-crafted, and thoughtful essay that includes all three components. So, let's focus on the three steps that will allow you to do that: Analysis, Structure, and Story.

Step 1: Analysis

Analysis is the basis on which you are able to share your story and make it acceptable to the reader. It's not your thesis or your statement. Analysis is the data that backs up your statement. It's the research that makes your statement viable.

For example, if you were to make the statement "I'm a considerate human being," you'd have to back that up. You need the data that reinforces your words in order for your words to be accepted as true by your reader. Just saying it isn't enough. You have to give examples as to why it's true. (Advanced writing would also give counterpoints, but we aren't going to address that in this book.)

Analysis comes in two forms: Objective and Subjective. For the purposes of this book, we'll use the house example from the last chapter. But for a moment, let's go back to the statement "I'm a considerate human being." A lot of people think of themselves as considerate, but in order for the reader to believe it, you'd have to have objective data that supports that statement, such as evidence of your volunteer work, and subjective data, such as opinions from friends or family.

It's this combination of data—or Analysis—that gives your essay the basis it needs to be acceptable or viable.

Objective and Subjective Data

Let's start by looking at objective data. What exactly is objective data? Objective data is fact. It's something that's true for everyone. If you were to buy a plot of land to build your house, you would come up with the same data as everyone else. Such as:

- There are boulders that need to be moved for the foundation.
- There is a tree that is in the way of the driveway.
- The land is elevated.
- The land is in a flood plain.
- The land requires drainage or irrigation.
- The soil has a high, or low, Ph value.

Anybody looking at this piece of land will have the same objective data, which will be verifiable. The truth is not altered by perspective or opinion. It is the same for everyone, which means everyone will accept it upon reading it.

Subjective data is different. Subjective data is unique to the individual, because it's based in perspective. An individual's perspective will skew their opinion in favor of or against something.

For example, a boulder being in the way of a foundation is a fact. What to do with the boulder will be subjective. People will have different emotional reactions to the facts. Their reactions are subjective based on their life's experiences, not the facts.

For some people the boulder might be a huge issue that needs solving, leading to frustration and stress. For other people they could see this as an opportunity to add a boulder to their landscape plan and create more visual interest in their garden. These two data points—a frustration and a gift—are subjective; yet both are true, because they're true for the individual making them.

Subjective analysis is often based on how something makes you feel. It's your opinion and your perspective. Objective data is devoid of feeling—it simply is, regardless of how you might feel about it. The boulder is in the ground where the foundation needs to go: Fact. The boulder is a nuisance, or the boulder is a gift: Opinion.

To better understand how to use Analysis to build the foundation of your essay, it's easiest to put your data—or research—in two lists as you are collecting it.

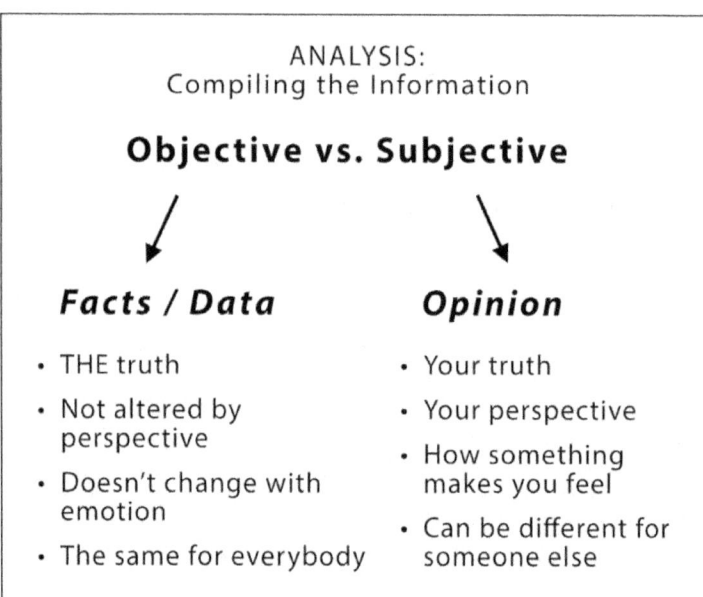

In order to compile your information, you have to have selected your topic, knowing of course that your focus might shift slightly as it did for the swimmer I discussed earlier in the book. Once you have identified your topic, you begin by writing down all the factual pieces: your objective data.

Objective Data

I like to start with the factual pieces, because more often than not we tend to believe something is factual—or objective—when it's actually not. Here's a simple example:

When I created this program, I gave a presentation to a local organization. I used pizza as the example and asked the attendees to give me objective data about pizza. For the purposes of keeping it as clear as possible, I said it was "Domino's plain cheese pizza."

Initially, these were the responses I received when I asked for a list of factual truths about the pizza:

Round	Greasy
Dough	Cheap
Cheese	Simple
Sauce	Healthy
Hot	Easy
Delicious	

Now, some of these are, in fact, objective data points. I think when we are talking about a "Domino's plain cheese pizza," we can mostly agree that it has sauce, dough, and cheese. Where we start to get into trouble is when we say that it is *factually* round, because I didn't specify a size, and I think some Domino's chains have a rectangular one. Additionally, I didn't say if it was cooked, so maybe it's not hot. Alternatively, maybe it's a leftover and it's cold from the refrigerator. For some people it might be cheap, and for others it might be a stretch financially. When you're a college student paying your own bills, a cheese pizza might be a luxury.

It also may, or may not, be simple, greasy, delicious, healthy, and easy. It all depends on your perspective. If you're eating ramen noodles every day, this might be a delicious and healthy (or healthier) alternative. If you're eating quinoa bowls filled with fresh or steamed vegetables, a Domino's pizza might be the least healthy thing you eat all week.

The truth is, there are a lot of things that we often attribute to being objective that actually aren't when we start to scratch beneath the surface. Additionally, when you have someone reading your essay for the first time, you can't make assumptions that they will think like you do.

I think that's one of the most important take-aways I would like to impress upon you: You can't ever assume that the person reading your essay knows what you are talking about. I address this again later in the book, but let's pause and look at it here as well.

For example, you may love horseback riding and use language that is unique to that sport. Or you may love swimming, basketball, or physics. The admissions officer may know absolutely nothing about any of those things, and so your objective data needs to speak to a base level of knowledge, truth, and acceptance about your specific topic. Your subjective data then invites them into your world by sharing your personal thoughts and opinions.

Subjective Data

When we carry the pizza example forward to look at subjective data, these are some possible responses:

Gooey	Flavorful
Filling	Bland
Disgusting	Mild
Spicy	Gross

By now, I think you get the picture. What *you* think about Domino's plain cheese pizza and what someone *else* thinks about Domino's plain cheese pizza will always be subjective. Your response will be based on your tastes, experience, and perspective.

To make it even more complex, having grown up near New York City, I often get into an argument with my Chicago friends about what even constitutes the word "pizza." When you add my Italian friends into the mix, it can really get interesting and even the seemingly objective data is up for grabs.

What matters when you are conducting your analysis is that you understand that there are two types of data (objective and subjective) and that the objective data makes your story accessible, viable, and relatable, while the subjective data is what makes your story more compelling. The two combined is what shows your reader that you have done the work to actually be making the statement you are making.

Step 2: Structure

If you're in my generation, you were taught how to create an arc in all of your writing by using these three categories:

Beginning — Middle — End

In general, this arc still holds true today, though I am not sure if it's still taught. I was a drama major in college, and we used the same premise. It's the backbone of all good storytelling. You want to have an inciting or catalyst moment (beginning), a plot (middle), and a resolution (end). Of course, it's not always as simple as that, as good creative writing often has numerous plot lines or arcs, but for a 500-600 word essay, you want to keep it as simple and clear as possible using this basic method.

For your college essay, you will want to have a beginning (your statement), a middle (the analysis of your statement), and an end (a meaningful result reinforcing your statement). If we go back to the statement "I'm a considerate human being," we would use the beginning to address who you are, the middle to give examples of how, and/or where you have been thoughtful, and the end to state why it matters or what it means.

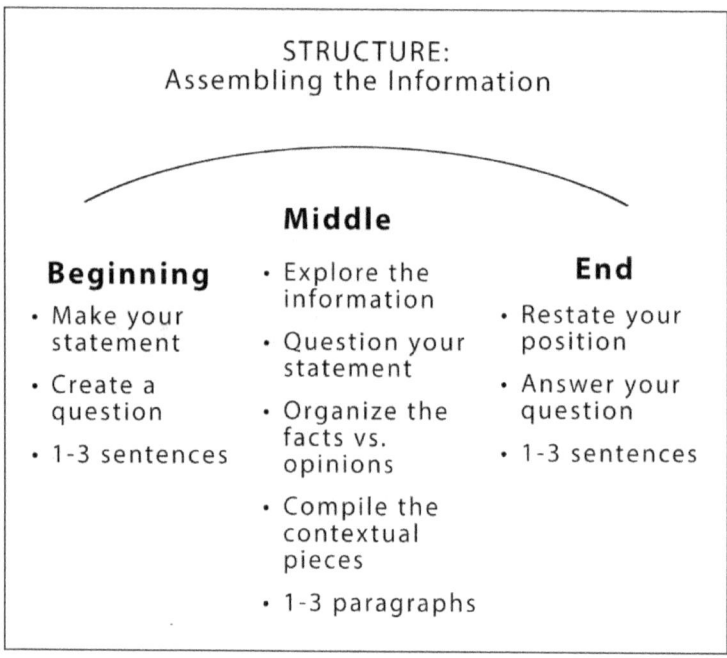

The structure needs to be in place for you to share your story. It's the walls of your house. You can't hang a painting on a wonky wall, because it won't look right. Nor can you place furniture on a slanted floor, as it won't be level or comfortable to use. Structure is what gives people access to your story. When it's done correctly, they won't notice it's there. When it's absent, it becomes an obstacle, and they won't be able to read your words.

So, how do you create structure once you've completed your analysis?

You start with your original statement, and then you ask a question and create 1-3 sentences around the answer. Let's look at the pizza again. An original statement about pizza could be: "I find that pizza is more than just a quick way to have a meal, because it creates moments of gathering."

In this instance, we are making a statement that pizza is about more than just food. In order to emphasize that statement we would want to ask a question, such as: How does pizza play a role in getting people together? We then would build 1-3 more sentences that state clearly what we are trying to convey, such as:

> *I find that pizza is more than just a quick way to have a meal, because it creates moments of gathering. Over the past two years, whenever pizza has been present at one of our social groups or organizations, meeting attendance has increased. This has led to more participation and more connection among my peers, which I have enjoyed and learned from.*

In this opening paragraph, we have made it clear that we are writing about pizza as the catalyst that has helped to bring together peer groups, which has directly impacted the author, seemingly in a positive way. We have not talked about the ingredients, or whether it was gooey or greasy; instead we have focused on pizza as a subject that has resulted in something unexpected, yet welcome. This is how we can take something as seemingly benign as pizza and turn it into a life-changing essay.

Note: This is also why you want to complete *all* of the steps before you begin writing, because in this example we would now have to go back to step 1 and do more analysis on why or how pizza can be used as a tool to develop community.

Once you have the necessary analysis, you can begin to work on building the middle part of the structure. This is where I am going to reiterate a very important point:

People don't read the same way they hear—so you shouldn't write the same way you speak.

I know I've already mentioned this, and I will mention it again in the next chapter, and probably once more at the end of the book. Step 2 is not the time to be writing full sentences, anyway. You're still building and crafting your essay. This is the time for using bullet points. In the middle section of your essay, you want to make a list of all the things you want to say, without actually writing them out yet.

This means that you will take your analysis and create bullet points from it. You may want to begin to link things together that make sense, and you may want to use things that oppose one another to make your point even clearer. When you are building your house, you have to know where the floors are in order to build the walls. You also have to know where your doorways, stairs, and windows will go in order to build your walls. This is not about throwing up walls and calling it done. It's about assessing everything you need to do and then how you are going to bring it all together.

The problem is that many of the essays I helped my young clients with were full of information at this point, but they often made no sense. To begin with, most of them were written the way we speak, which meant they were often rambling and had poor grammar. Here is what they all had in common:

- There was no clear arc.

- There was no obvious reason as to why things were being said or what they had to do with the main statement.

- There were just statements of analysis, which were often repetitive or redundant. (Did you see what I did there?)

- There was no story, even though they were filled with personal anecdotes and opinions.

In order to have a solid middle section, you have to lay out all the pieces and rearrange them in an order that tells a story. Your story exists because of this step. If you are bouncing around making comparisons that don't make sense, or sharing your opinions and experiences without a clear context, nobody is going to be engaged in your essay.

For a 500-600 word essay, you probably want to plan on having three paragraphs. If we use the pizza example again, that might look like this:

> Paragraph 1: *Focus on objective analysis, while also mentioning something subjective*
>
> - Which organizations, specifically?
>
> - How many people showed up with pizza vs. without?
>
> - How often were these meetings?

- Begin to mention noticing the difference and how it affected you.

Paragraph 2: *Focus on subjective analysis, with some objective statements*

- What was your participation in these meetings?
- How did you feel when there was pizza?
- How did you feel when there were more participants?
- What changed for you as a result?

Paragraph 3: *Focus on subjective analysis, and mention hypothesized conclusion*

- Why would you use pizza as a meeting tool in the future?
- Why *wouldn't* you use pizza as a meeting tool in the future?
- What can you discern from using pizza as a meeting tool in the future?
- How did you realize more connection and enjoyment as a result?

These are just ideas, of course, but they are a place to start. In the middle section of your essay, you want to focus on all the things that support and validate your original statement. You also want to place them in an order that makes sense and gives you an arc. Only then can you write a conclusion that wraps up your essay.

The conclusion should be a reiteration of your original statement, with an insight (result) attached. Remember, this is about showing the admissions officer *who* you are—your character. The addition of an insight is what will stay with them after your 5 minutes and 500 words are up.

You want to keep the end of your essay positively-focused. This is not a time to introduce a disclaimer or a qualifying statement. This is a time to stand firmly in your boots and re-introduce yourself to your reader.

The final paragraph should have about 1-3 sentences, and should answer the original question posed by the essay prompt. It should leave the reader knowing who you are *and* wanting to go deeper and get to know you more.

- Sentence 1: *Reiterate your original statement in a new way*

    o Answer the original essay question or prompt.

    o Make a point of saying the same thing you already said, but in a new way.

- Sentence 2: *Add a statement about why that's important*

    o Ask yourself *why* this was important to you, and answer that question.

- - Why did you choose this topic to write about?

- Sentence 3: *Finish by stating how you will carry this information forward*

  - - Think of the future and how you can apply whatever you learned in a new way.

  - - Describe how this has changed you forever and will impact your future.

Ultimately, you want an interview. You want the admissions officer to say: "This is someone we want to know better," or "This is someone we want in our school." Your essay can do this when you use the three steps to put your best foot forward.

Of course, your Story is the main access point for Everybody reading your essay. If the Analysis falls short, or your Structure is weak, it becomes increasingly difficult for the admissions officer to read your Story.

However, if the Analysis is complete and the Structure is intact, the admissions officer will *only* read your Story, which is exactly what you want.

So, what's your Story?

Step 3: Story

I believe everyone has a story in them, if not several. We were born storytellers. It's in our DNA. Even before the advent of writing, we told each other stories. The various prehistoric cave paintings discovered around the world are proof of this simple fact.

When we're talking about adding the Story to your essay, we're talking about adding those pieces that give it meaning. This is the narrative that answers these essential questions:

- Why does this matter?

- Why should someone care?

- What do I want them to care about?

- How do I want them to feel when they read my words?

- What is my desired outcome?

> **STORY:**
> **Adding the Narrative**
>
> **When?** **Why?**
> **How?** **Purpose?**
>   **Meaning?**
> **Where?** **Who?**
>
> > Why does this matter?
> > Why should someone care?
> > What should someone care about?
> > How do you want them to feel when they read your words?
> > What is your desired outcome?

The Story is not the walls or the floors—it is the paint that goes on the walls, and, more specifically, the color. It's the carpet or tile, the paintings and art you hang, the bed linens, and throw pillows on your sofa. It's what makes your proverbial house a home. It's what makes it *your* home.

The Story includes all the little details that validate and support your original statement. It includes the experiences, thoughts, beliefs, "a-ha!" moments, and anecdotes from your life.

The Story is where you get to show your character.

One of my young clients used a story of resilience and innovation for his college essay. When he started crafting it and assembling all the building blocks, he was not focused on conveying resilience or innovation. He only wanted to share an experience in his life that he thought might be interesting and show that he had a perspective shift. Ultimately, it became a story about resilience and innovation, though he never stated that overtly, because it's what all the details showed.

About a year prior to writing, he had sustained a rather serious injury. Instead of listening 100% to the doctor's advice (which would have had him laid up for three months), he decided to look for other options. He didn't want to cause further harm to himself, but he also didn't agree with lying in bed or on a sofa for 90 days doing essentially nothing.

What did he do?

He looked for opportunities to modify his way of doing things, in order to continue to participate as much as possible in his life and enjoy the things that made him happy. He didn't accept the label of "limited" that was given to him. Instead, he chose to create his own label of "creative," which allowed him to find different solutions to his new problem of decreased mobility.

In his essay, he proposed an original statement about a recent challenge he faced becoming an unexpected opportunity. As he went on, he used all the various data points about this challenge and what he did to accommodate it. In the end, he reiterated how proud he felt to have overcome this challenge in his life.

What he didn't realize he was doing was sharing with the admissions officer the following statements about his character. He was: resilient, innovative, optimistic, resourceful, creative, patient, motivated, and thoughtful.

He never flatly stated he was "resilient," or that he "learned how to be resilient." He *showed* resilience in his story. He never said, "I'm innovative." He described his ability to be creative and thoughtful. He didn't write, "I feel I was resourceful in my approach to the problem." He shared the things he did that conveyed an ability to find other ways of doing something—which shows how resourceful he is.

When you're telling your story, you use words to show what you want the reader to infer. If you describe something that shows strength, your reader will make the assessment that you are strong. If you write about your volunteer work with orphaned animals and how it has positively affected your life, your reader will infer that you are compassionate.

This is why we use Story as the final step. We want our reader to relate to us through common character traits, without telling them what to think.

Of course, Story is the access point for Everyone. This means that it has to be good. "Good" is a subjective word, though. What is "good" when telling a story? In my opinion, "good" translates to "meaningful."

In order to make your story meaningful, it has to be unique to you. Everyone on a swim team should be able to tell a different story about the same event, because, presumably, they would all have had slightly different experiences.

Stories include specifics or detailed information. The Analysis and the Structure don't have this level of detail. If you were to write about pizza at group meetings, you might focus on how nice it was to see so many people laughing and smiling as they enjoyed the pizza. To make it more personal and meaningful, you might say something like:

> "I was having a difficult day as I had just received some disappointing news from my family, but when I got to the group meeting and saw everyone connecting around the pizza box, laughing, smiling, and sharing stories—both good and bad—about their days, I suddenly felt a little bit better. I realized I wasn't the only one going through a stressful time, and somehow that box of baked dough, sauce, and cheese made everything better for everyone in the room, even if it was only for a little while."

By adding the personal anecdotes and "window dressing," you are creating moments of connection with another person. This is why those Story questions in the diagram are so important. You want the reader to care about you, connect with you, and feel invested in you through what you've written.

By bringing in pieces from your life that make it real and tangible, you create these opportunities for connection. The Story is not only the element that highlights your character, it's what makes your character real. You want the reader to be able to imagine the person in front of them whose words they are reading on a page.

Ultimately, you're asking someone to read about you. The story you choose to share—the topic you choose to write about—says, "this matters to me." From there, you can either focus on why it's important to you, or focus on why you want it to be important to them.

A good story will address either of these aspects. A good essay— the *perfect* essay— will accomplish both.

Tripping Yourself Up

If you've done all the steps, you've compiled your data, built a roadmap to follow, and crafted your essay using personal anecdotes, you're well on your way to having the *perfect* college essay. There are a few places, however, where you can trip yourself up without realizing it. Unfortunately, this can undo some of your hard work.

What do I mean by "trip yourself up" in relation to your hard work? Well, let me tell you a story from when I served as an alumni interviewer for my college that highlights one of the obstacles you can face when writing your college essay.

Don't Use Fancy Words

Once a year, my alma mater would send me three or four students that lived in my area to be interviewed. They had made it past the first round, and the college was interested in getting to know them better. A lot of people can't travel to conduct on-campus interviews, so that alumni network chips in and helps by conducting in-home interviews on their behalf.

I did this for a number of years, and every year there was at least one applicant who tripped themselves up by doing something they shouldn't have done. The most obvious was the use of fancy words.

Typically, when I'm working with a young client on their college essays, if there is a fancy word in the midst of their writing, I ask them about it. I do this, because, more often than not, their well-intentioned parent has suggested it or added it for them. As a writer, it stands out like a Great Dane in a line of Chihuahuas. When I'm working with them, I advise them to change it back to their own language.

As an interviewer, however, I would manage to use it in conversation in order to see if it was their word or not. Too often, they didn't know what the word meant. Now, I never wrote to my school that the person shouldn't be offered admission as a result, but it did give me an insight into their character when I called them on it. Some would nervously laugh and say it was their parents' idea, and we'd have a good chuckle about it and move on. Inevitably, the interview would always be more enjoyable after that.

Others, however, would insist that they knew what it meant (they just forgot in that moment), and then they would double-down on using fancier words in the interview itself. Personally, I don't care what your vocabulary is, and most admissions officers don't either. We care about who you are, whether you're a good fit for the school, and whether the school is a good fit for you.

Of course, the exception to the rule is when you're using language specific to a program you're interested in, such as STEM. In those cases, use all the big words, just be sure you can back them up.

There are other ways you can trip yourself up as well, such as: 1) don't assume your reader knows what you mean, 2) don't overshare, and 3) don't forget to edit, then edit again. And again.

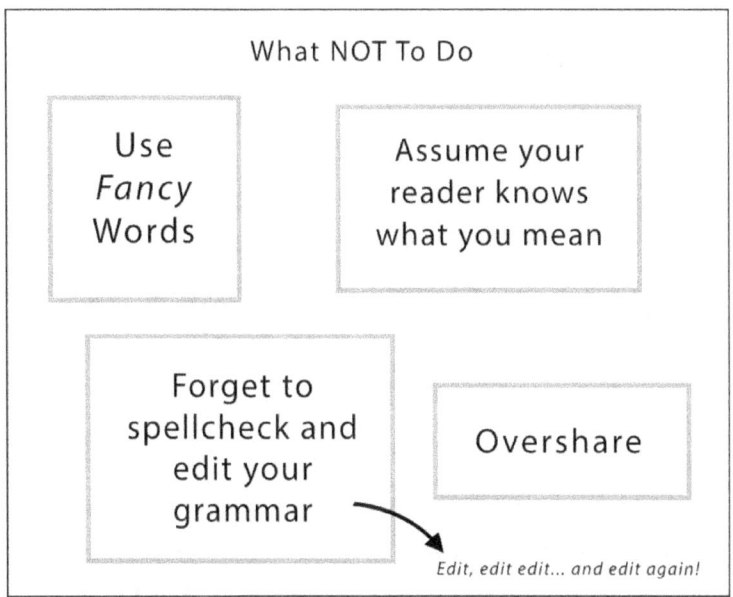

Don't Overshare

Oversharing is one of those areas where it can get a little tricky. On the one hand, you want to be personal enough with your story that the admissions officer feels like they know you. On the other hand, you don't want to use drama to make a connection, because it rarely shows character. In other words, if you have a traumatic story that you are using for your essay, it's better to focus on how it affected you and the positive (hopefully) results than it is to focus on the drama.

Additionally, there are certain buzz words that students use to convey a sense of learning, growth, or resilience. If you're saying, "I really grew from that experience," explain how. If you want, "That experience made me a better person," then you're using a phrase ("better person") that doesn't actually say much. Again, let the reader infer that you are a better person because of what you wrote in your story. Don't tell them you are. False humility, false modesty, and false bravado are very easily recognized.

Be real, be authentic, and, above all, be yourself.

This leads us to another obstacle you can face that I have already alluded to in a previous chapter.

Don't Assume

If you're writing about something seemingly common, such as eating pizza, you can make a few assumptions that the admissions officer could relate to that experience. If, however, you are writing about something less common, such as singing in an elite choir, you want to be sure to write your essay using language that makes that experience accessible without assuming the reader knows what you're talking about. Even though most people listen to music, not everyone has had the experience of singing in a choir, let alone an elite choir.

When I was writing this section of the book, I was actually going to use an example of playing the tuba. However, since I have never played the tuba, there is no way I can write about it. Knowing your limitations in your writing is important. So, instead of writing about the tuba, I switched it to writing about singing in an elite choir.

When I was in high school, I was a member of a 16-girl choir. We were "elite" in that we practiced every day, which meant it was a full course. We also were hired for private events, especially during the holidays, and we even sang a mass in the Duomo in Florence. The highlight for me, though, was singing at the staff Christmas party at the White House.

If I were to write about that event in my college essay, I would have to use a portion of the 500 words to explain what I just wrote in the last paragraph. I could never assume that the admissions officer would know what it means to "sing in an elite choir." So, I have to be able to allot a portion of my word count to giving some background or explanation. (By the way, that last paragraph was 68 words: more than 10% of my essay. You'll want to be careful about choosing your topic if you know that you have to explain things a bit more.)

Finally, there is one aspect of essay writing that needs to be emphasized above all others: Editing.

Edit, Edit, Edit... and Edit Again!

You could have the best story, with a strong structure, based on solid analysis, but if you have typos and grammatical errors, you are undermining your work. One of the fastest ways to exclude yourself from opportunity is to diminish the importance of editing.

Actually, there's no excuse for spelling mistakes in this day and age. Every word processing program has a built-in spelling checker. However, it's also something you should not rely on solely. Just because something is spelled correctly does not mean it's correct. Notice these two sentences:

- I took the dog for a walk out side today.

- I took the dog for a walk outside today.

Or how about this?

- To make it more persona and meaningful, you might say something like:

- To make it more personal and meaningful, you might say something like:

You actually just read that sentence in the last chapter. When I initially wrote it, it was the first bullet point with the word "persona" (not "personal"), which spell check didn't catch. Editing did.

There are no actual spelling mistakes in any of those examples; however, one is correct and one is not. Or how about these actual mistakes from a paper I edited:

> "The point of the event was to bring together people of different backgrounds, people who went to make a difference, and who new what it meant to be apart of something bigger."

Where are the errors? There are two obvious ones ("new" and "apart") and one questionable one ("went to"). As it turned out, the author meant to say "wanted to" instead of "went to." and there is no way a program would catch that.

A lot of word processing programs now include grammatical corrections, but they're not always correct. They infer what you are trying to say, based on all the data they have collected over the years. However, they can't always know what you mean. Sometimes the suggestion they make will completely change the tone of a sentence or its meaning.

Small errors like this don't show someone that you don't know how to spell (though they can). They show someone that you don't pay attention to detail. The message an admissions officer is receiving from an essay with typos and errors is that you aren't invested in yourself, because you didn't take the time to edit properly and make the corrections.

Of course, nobody is immune from typos and errors. Nearly every day I read something online that has an error. If you pull up any major media outlet, like a blog, online magazine, or articles, there is almost always an error somewhere. Personally, I always wonder how it got past the editors, but it does.

Recently, I published an internal document for my company that I thought had been edited. Five people had reviewed it for content over a period of a month. When it got to the last person, they commented that it was missing a "." on certain bullet points, which wasn't necessarily grammatically incorrect, however, it was inconsistent with the rest of the document.

Thankfully, when I went in to fix those bullet points, I noticed there were a few more inconsistencies. I took the time to read it again; but this time, I wasn't reading it for the content, I was reading it one word at a time, just in case. I caught at least seven more places where there were typos.

These were the things that went under the radar screen of the word processing program. They are little mistakes that maybe someone wouldn't notice, but why take that risk?

The advice is to have every essay you want to submit edited by at least three different people. So many people are willing to edit and help you, especially when it's for your college application. Make sure it's someone you trust, of course, before you hand them your essay.

I often suggest that you ask: a parent, a teacher, and another adult (such as a counselor or coach) before you ask a friend. They may be in the same boat as you, and wouldn't necessarily have the skills to help you properly.

After you have edited it once, and had someone else look at it, I have two small tips for you:

1. Because it's only about 500-600 words, read it one more time yourself, *from the bottom up*. When you read it backwards, you're more likely to catch the little spelling mistakes, because you're not reading content or story, you're reading words; and

2. Read it aloud. When you read something out loud, you have to slow down. We speak much more slowly than we

read. By slowing down, you may catch other tiny typos that you missed when you were just reading it silently in your head.

Finally, I think the biggest pattern I saw among all the essays I read by my young clients is something I've already mentioned twice: Writing as they speak.

Since the advent of texting and all the social media apps, our society has created shortcuts in our communication style. This has resulted in those shortcuts being transferred to writing, and it doesn't work. I have already shared this in Step 2, and I restate it here. What you need to remember is this:

People don't read the same way they listen or hear; therefore, you shouldn't write the same way you speak.

It's also true in the reverse.

I can't tell you the number of times I have heard a speech, or listened to a sermon, that was clearly written as an article without ever being read aloud. It becomes equally as distracting to have to listen to something that is supposed to be read.

Of course, there is one area of writing that requires both: Speechwriting.

Speechwriting is a style of writing that is incredibly specific, and good speechwriters make a lot of money for their craft. It requires blending speech pattern with listening pattern, analysis with story, and a unique structure with proper writing.

What matters for you in writing your college essay is remembering that someone is going to be reading it, and often in less than five minutes. If you're not writing for that purpose, you're missing an opportunity.

Putting It All Together

Crafting the *Perfect* College Essay is about compiling all the components before you begin writing. It's about knowing what you want to say, how you want to say it, and why it matters before you actually start typing. There is no shortcut to writing well; however, as you have now learned, there are specific steps you can take that will help you develop into a great writer.

By using this method and following these steps, you will be able to create an essay that is both compelling and accessible. Your essay will have a strong foundation supporting a meaningful story. To follow is an outline you can use as a checklist for building your essay:

1. Make your statement
2. Compile your analysis in two lists:
    a. Objective points
    b. Subjective points

3. Craft bullet points from your analysis by asking deeper questions
   a. Link ideas or themes together
   b. Remove redundancies
   c. Group bullet points in an arc, based on story progression

4. Add your personal anecdotes to the story
   a. Identify specific examples for each of your bullet points
   b. Share your thoughts/ideas as a result of the analysis

5. Revisit your original statement to make sure it is still accurate

6. Identify a meaningful insight related to your statement

Your college essay is effective when you engage the reader in a single aspect of your life, so much so that they want to meet you. The goal of the college essay is to leave the admissions officer wanting more—enough to invite you to interview. It is a single (and brief!) opportunity to show them who you are and why you are a great fit for their school.

Most importantly, once you begin to understand this process, it can be honed and used throughout the rest of your life. Writing well is something you can practice in many different areas of your life, from school to work, to communication, and more. Literally, there isn't a day that goes by that you won't read something that someone else has written. Whether it's a sign on the back of a bus, a book for a class, or an instruction manual for a new set of speakers, someone has written it.

In short, learning how to write well is an important skill that will carry you forward into any career you choose.

About Me and Why I Wrote This Book

In order to understand how this all came together, I thought I would share a little about myself. My hope is that you will gain a deeper understanding of why this program works and how I came to develop it. Most people change careers at least three times in their life. Me? I changed careers seven times in three decades, but they all had two things in common: 1) I was always helping people in some way, and 2) I was always writing and creating.

My path to today was varied and, at times, difficult, and I wouldn't change it for anything. It has taught me more than I could ever have learned any other way. My toolbox is overflowing, which allows me to see things from many different perspectives. It was these experiences that contributed to me creating this writing program.

For almost five years, I helped young writers with their college essays. More often than not, it was a child of a client or someone I knew. Sometimes it was even a family member. I really enjoyed seeing their writing change over the course of several months, as a result of teaching them *how* to write. The subject didn't matter, because this three-step approach can be used in almost any situation, and that made everything easier.

Over the years, I noticed a pattern with everyone I worked with that was a huge stumbling block to good writing: Everyone was writing as if they were speaking. As we have already discussed, this is a problem for one main reason: *People don't read the same way they hear.*

This told me that I had to go back to basics with each of these young writers and change the focus of their approach. Instead of writing, I had to teach them how to *craft* an essay.

Now, because I am a Certified Life Coach, I also know how to help people shift their perspective and gain more clarity in their lives. I could use these tools to help my teenage clients better understand what it was they were trying to accomplish.

By combining my knowledge as a life coach and professional writer, I created a simple strategy that is accessible to anyone. Whether you are 15 or 50, you can use this approach to write anything. The essay length doesn't matter. You can even use this three-step model if you are writing a 20-page research paper, because it focuses on *how* to write.

If you are wondering why I decided to share a chapter on my experience and why I chose to write this book, let me tell you a story about myself and my path to understanding writing.

When I was a senior in high school, we had a new English teacher. Up until that point I had gotten by in my writing by relying on my voice—my opinions. I wouldn't have called myself a great writer, but I was passionate. My new teacher took my first essay and handed it back to me. He said something like, "You have no analysis in here. It's all voice." He didn't even give me a grade.

I had to take the essay back and redo the whole thing. This was before computers, so I re-wrote all five pages by hand. This was the first time somebody called me out on my writing. He wasn't focused on the content; he was focused on the style. At the time, I didn't understand that fully. However, throughout that year, I learned from him how to write with analysis.

Then I went to college.

During my first semester, my English professor assigned us an essay on Joseph Conrad's *Heart of Darkness*. I wrote a beautiful essay exploring all the themes in the book and handed it in. My professor called me to his office and said, "I'm going to give you another shot at this." I paused before slowly replying, "All right..."

He continued.

"You have absolutely no voice in here. This is all analysis. I read the book; I don't need analysis. I'm wondering what you thought of it. How did it make you feel? What's your perspective?"

His feedback directly contradicted what I had just spent an entire year learning with my high school teacher. In less than 14 months, I had two experts in their field give me opposing advice. Of course, I rewrote the essay and turned it in, and I received an A- for tardiness (not something they always tell you upfront).

I was frustrated. I didn't understand how one could want one thing, and one could want the other. So, I spent my freshman year learning how to find my voice again and add it to the analysis.

In the end, I learned that to write well and to convey a story, you have to have both. You have to have a voice that's unique to you, but it has to be grounded in analysis. In order to tell a story, there has to be a foundation. You can't have one or the other, you need both.

By knowing *how* to do something and doing it well, people are more likely to stick around for the *why*. It's one of the tenets of this program. If your foundation is strong, nobody will notice it, and they will hear the story and your message. However, if your foundation is weak, most people will give up before ever getting to the story. That's why it's so important to craft first, write second.

Now it's your turn to put these steps to use to craft your best essay: the *perfect* college essay.

Good luck!

Crafting the Perfect College Essay

Acknowledgements

Over the years, I have had many people help me hone my craft. Of course, I need to acknowledge the two professors I referred to in the final chapter: Jeffrey Schwartz and Ted Mason. Together, without realizing it, they taught me more about writing than I could have acknowledged at the time.

I also want to thank my go-to editors: Sally Abbey and Taylor Wray who always double-check my work and consistently challenge me to be a better writer and storyteller. Additionally, I would like to thank Phoebe Jacoby and Grace Sanko for their hard work and valuable contributions to bringing this material to life.

Finally, to the many students and young people I have helped over the years, this book, workbook, and program are a result of our work together. Thank you for your part in inspiring me to create a system that anyone anywhere can use to improve their essay-writing skills. My hope is that this will take the fear out of writing and help to create a world with more storytellers.

Resources

There are numerous writing resources available in print and online—too many to list, actually. For the most part, they are organized by genre. One of the best ways to improve your writing over time is by joining a good writing group.

Additionally, there are many writing-related magazines that you can use to continually hone your craft. Some of the ones I have used include: *Writer's Digest, Poets & Writers,* and *Publishers Weekly.* They offer a lot of information about the business of writing, as well as a lot of resources.

In order to make the essay-writing process even easier, I have created a 28-page companion workbook that has all the exercises you will need to craft your best college essay. When used in conjunction with this book, it guides you through the step-by-step process in real time. To follow are a few example pages from the workbook.

The best part is, you don't have to wait. You can purchase and download the workbook right away at Inspirebytes.com.

Thank you, and good luck with your essay!

EXAMPLE PAGE 1

Crafting the *Perfect* College Essay   The Workbook

6. What are you passionate about?

   a. _____

   b. _____

   c. _____

With your topics listed above, it's time to decide what you want to write about.

Exercise #3: Look at the list above and see what jumps out at you the most, or where your ideas have overlapped and are listed more than once. Because you have written it more than one time, it is probably meaningful to you. This is something you might want to focus on for your essay. Write it down.

TOPIC: _____

Now write a sentence about this topic.

_____

_____

You will use this topic and/or sentence for the rest of the exercises in this workbook so that you can build the pieces of your essay as you go along.

Martina E. Faulkner LMSW

EXAMPLE PAGE 2

Crafting the *Perfect* College Essay — The Workbook

Now answer these yes/no questions:

- Do these points tell you enough that you feel like you know him or her? [YES / NO]
- If you were an admissions officer, would you want to invite this person for an interview? [YES / NO]
- Would this person stand out from the crowd and the rest of the essays? [YES / NO]

In my assessment, I would say that this person enjoyed joining many organizations throughout their high school years; however, I do not know

- What the actual clubs were;
- How much time was spent with each organization; and
- Why the author chose the clubs/organizations.

It's one thing to say you joined a club. It's quite different when you say what club it was, why you joined it, what you learned, where it met, and how it has affected you.

Exercise #5: Using your TOPIC, list details that answer the 'Who-What-Where-How-Why' questions.

Who
_____

What
_____

Where
_____

How
_____

Why
_____

Now that you have the basics identified, we can start to work on the three steps you need to craft your essay. They are:

Analysis   Structure   Story

© 2020 Martina E. Faulkner, LMSW. All Rights Reserved.

EXAMPLE PAGE 3

Crafting the *Perfect* College Essay   The Workbook

How do you add story to your structure and analysis?

This is where you get to use specific examples and personal details that support your original statement. These are the elements that "show" your statement to be true, instead of simply stating it. For example, in the bad essay about joining lots of clubs, we changed the original statement to: "I joined many clubs throughout high school, but one stood out above the rest."

In order for this to be true, we would have to add personal details that align with our analysis and answer the questions we posed in the structure. This is also where we get to add a conclusion that carries the story forward into the potential future and simultaneously reinforces the original statement in a new way.

In order to make your story meaningful, it has to be unique to you. By bringing in pieces from your life that make it real and tangible, you create opportunities for connection. The anecdotes you choose to share (just like the topic you choose to write about) says, "this matters to me."

Adding the story is as simple as thinking of examples from your life that match the pieces we identified in Exercise #9.

Exercise #10: Identify real-life examples. For each of your questions from Exercise #9 (the Beginning/Middle/End), make a note about a story from your life. It's alright if these overlap.

BEGINNING Question Story:

MIDDLE Question #1 Story:

MIDDLE Question #2 Story:

About the Author

Martina E. Faulkner, LMSW is an author, publisher, certified life coach, licensed therapist, and Reiki Master Teacher. Unique in her approach to helping others, Martina's work transcends any one method or genre and offers something entirely new.

In her writing, Martina draws on her distinctive experience allowing her to be the best possible guide and teacher for her clients. Through her various programs and books, whether fiction, nonfiction, poetry, or children's (published as Tia Martina), Martina's focus is always on providing hope, opportunity, perspective, and a little bit of fun!

When she isn't writing, Martina likes to spend time with her dogs, friends, and family. A self-proclaimed Anglophile, Martina drinks tea daily and loves to look at beautiful images from the British Isles while daydreaming about her next book.

www.martinafaulkner.com
www.TiaMartina.com

Martina E. Faulkner LMSW

Other Books by the Author

What if..?
How to Create the Life You Want Using the Power of Possibility

Infinite In My Heart
Poems of Love, Loss, and Hope

Coming Soon

When the World Went Quiet
(September 2020)

What now..?
11 Simple Things You Can Do to Change Your Life
(December 2020)

For more information, please visit:

martinafaulkner.com
inspirebytes.com

www.ingramcontent.com/pod-product-compliance
Lightning Source LLC
Chambersburg PA
CBHW070739020526
44118CB00035B/1687